WHY RATS ALWAYS RUN AWAY ON SEEING THE OWNER OF THE HOUSE

BY

BISHOP OCHEI INNOCENT

Table of Contents

NOTE PLEASE:

All pictures used in this book are taken from the public domain.

THIS STORY TELLS WHY WE MUST NOT BEHAVE LIKE RATS.

THERE ARE SOME THINGS RATS DO THAT WE SHOULD NEVER DO.

WE MUST FIND OUT WHAT THOSE THINGS ARE AND WHAT THE BIBLE SAYS IS THE PUNISHMENT FOR THOSE WHO COMMIT THOSE SINS.

WHY RATS ALWAYS RUN AWAY

MOST RATS ARE THIEVES.

**THIEVES ENTER PEOPLES'
HOUSES WITHOUT
KNOCKING ON THE DOOR.**

A GOOD MAN KNOCKS BEFORE
ENTERING ANY HOUSE.

MOST THIEVES GO TO PEOPLES' HOME AT NIGHT

OR WHEN THEY ARE NOT IN.

**A RAT EQUALLY ENTERS
YOUR HOUSE AT NIGHT
AND/OR**

WITHOUT PERMISSION

**JUST LIKE HUMAN BEINGS,
NOT ALL RATS ARE
THIEVES.**

SOME ARE FRIENDLY LIKE THIS
TINY ONE ON THIS MAN'S LEG.

BUT MOST RATS ENTER
YOUR HOUSE TO STEAL
SOMETHING TO EAT

SOME RATS AFTER EATING
BECOME VERY FAT LIKE
THIS ONE

**OTHERS NO MATTER WHAT
THEY EAT, REMAIN SLIM
LIKE THIS ONE**

NOT ALL RATS ARE BLACK AS YOU
CAN SEE FROM THE ONE ABOVE.

**WHETHER BLACK OR
YELLOW, THIEVES DO NOT
LIKE TO MEET WITH THE
OWNER OF THE HOUSE**

THEY ENTER WHEN HE IS NOT
THERE

WHEN SOME RATS DO NOT
FIND FOOD IN YOUR HOME,
THEY EAT YOUR
FURNITURE AS THIS ONE
BELOW IS DOING.

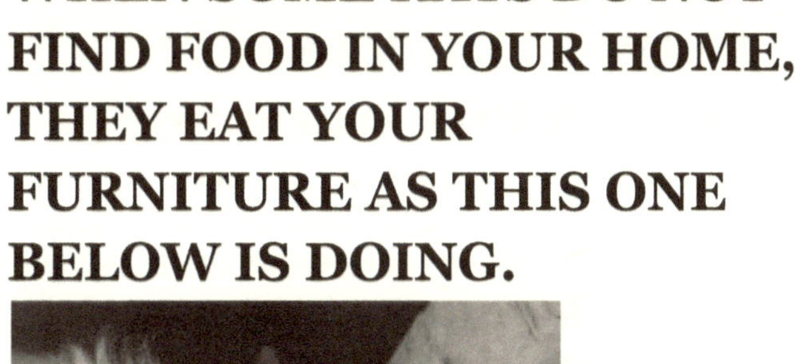

THE ONLY THING RATS

ARE PUSSY CATS.

THIS IS BECAUSE CATS EAT

RATS!

ANOTHER THING THAT EATS RATS ARE SNAKES.

SOME RATS LIVE IN BUSHES AROUND US.

AND FROM THERE SNEAK IN TO STEAL OUR FOOD.

**THAT IS WHY FOOD
SHOULD NEVER BE LEFT
WHERE RATS CAN REACH
THEM.**

THEY SHOULD RATHER BE KEPT IN
FRIDGES.

NOT ALL HOME OWNERS MIGHT WANT TO KILL A RAT. SOME MIGHT WANT TO CHASE IT AWAY.

SO GRANDMAS ARE TOO KIND TO HARM ANYBODY, INCLUDING THIEVES.

YET, ONCE RAT SNIFFS THE PRESENCE OF THE OWNER, IT RUNS AWAY.

DO YOU KNOW WHY THIS IS SO?

THE BIBLE SAYS:

"The wicked flee though no one pursues, but the righteous are as bold as a lion."

Proverbs 28:1

THEY RUN BECAUSE THE KNOW THAT WHAT THEY ARE DOING IS NOT GOOD.

A GOOD MAN WILL NEVER TAKE ANOTHER PERSON'S PROPERTY WITHOUT PERMISSION.

THIS IS SPECIALLY SO CONCERNING MONEY AND OTHER THINGS YOUR PARENTS LEAVE ON THE TABLE.

YOU MUST NOT TAKE THEM WITHOUT THEIR PERMISSION.

WHEN YOU TAKE WHAT IS NEITHER YOURS NOR GIVEN TO YOU, YOU ARE STEALING AND THIS IS WHAT THE BIBLE SAYS WILL HAPPEN TO THOSE WHO STEAL!

10 "Nor thieves nor the greedy nor drunkards nor slanderers nor swindlers will inherit the kingdom of God."

1 Corinth 6:10

THOSE WHO STEAL WILL NOT ENTER HEAVEN!

I KNOW YOU WILL LIKE TO GO
TO HEAVEN BECAUSE THAT IS
WHERE OUR GOD AND FATHER
IS LIVING!

ALL GOOD THINGS ARE THERE!

CAN YOU ANSWER THE FOLLOWING QUESTIONS?

1. WHY DO THIEVES NOT KNOCK ON DOORS? ....

2. WHAT DO RATS DO WHEN THEY ENTER YOUR HOUSE? ....

3. WHAT MAKES SOMEBODY A THIEF? ....

4. WHY DO THIEVES RUN AWAY
WHEN THEY SEE THE HOME
OWNER?.......................................
....
....
....
....

5. WILL THIEVES GO TO
HEAVEN?

....
....
....
....
....

6. WILL A DRUNKARD GET TO
HEAVEN?...................................
....
....
....
....

7. MENTION ONE THING YOU
LEARNT FROM THIS
BOOK?.......................................

THANK YOU
FOR READING THROUGH.

I PRAY THAT GOD WILL CONTINUE
TO BLESS YOU AND YOUR FAMILY.

I PRAY ALSO THAT YOU WILL
REMEMBER WHAT YOU READ IN
THIS BOOK.

THANKS SO MUCH, MY FRIEND.

-BISHOP OCHEI INNOCENT.

newochei@gmail.com

OTHER CHILDREN'S BOOK BY THE SAME AUTHOR

1. THE SAD STORY OF MRS. HEN.

2. TEN THINGS WE CAN LEARN FROM ANTS.

3. WHY RATS ALWAYS RUN AWAY ON SEEING THE OWNER OF THE HOUSE.

4. HOW GOD BLESSES PEOPLE

PARENTS' COMMENTS

ABOUT THE AUTHOR

BISHOP OCHEI INNOCENT IS THE PRESIDENT OF NEW DIMENSION SEMINARIES INTERNATIONAL.

HE LOVES TO REACH CHILDREN WITH ENTERTAINING AND TEACHING BIBLE STORIES.

GENERAL NOTES

GENERAL NOTES